LIBERTY
VS
POWER

THE FOUNDING FATHERS' VISION FOR AMERICA

TIMOTHY D. JOHNSON, PH.D.

Requests for information should be addressed to:
TRIG Publishing
4701 Chepstow Dr
Nashville, TN 37211

ISBN 978-1-4507-2761-7

Project Manager: Clay Young

Cover and interior design by Marc Whitaker / MTWdesign.net

Printed in the United States of America

Other titles by Timothy D. Johnson, Ph.D.

Winfield Scott: The Quest For Military Glory (1998)

A Fighter From Way Back: The Mexican War Diary of Lt. Daniel Harvey Hill (2002)

A Gallant Little Army: The Mexico City Campaign (2007)

Notes of the Mexican War, 1846-1848 (2010)

CONTENTS

INTRODUCTION

When I was in graduate school in the 1980s one of my professors said
that we could not find fifty-five Americans who could match the brains,
foresight, and wisdom of those who gathered in Philadelphia in the summer
of 1787 to devise our system of government. As a twenty something
year old young man, I thought to myself, yea sure. Over the years,
however, I have come to understand and appreciate that statement.
Despite divergent views and competing interests, our Founding Fathers
created a framework for government that is unparalleled in history. Their
achievement was so remarkable that one historian referred to it as "The
Miracle at Philadelphia" and another as "A Brilliant Solution."

Our Founding Fathers did not trust government, preferring instead to put
the country's future in the hands of a free, frugal, industrious, innovative
and virtuous people. They understood that a free and virtuous people
neither need nor want much government. From their study of history
and from their own experiences, they also understood that personal liberty
would survive only as long as government could be restrained. Thus, at
the Constitutional Convention they created a framework of government
that is limited by law. Throughout all ages there are certain unchanging
principles about government's relentless quest to possess more power.
Our Founding Fathers crafted a system that placed liberty above power.
They did so with the knowledge that citizens play the vital role in pre-
serving their own liberty in a free society.

Increasingly, Americans look to government to solve problems and provide the necessities of life. While government can solve some problems
and does have a role to play, it cannot provide all of our needs: neither

should it. The federal government is innately inefficient and clumsy, and major problems are better solved by the ingenuity of private citizens. In recent decades Americans seem to understand our founding principles less and less, and that is primarily because they have been exposed to them less and less. Many schools have forgotten the true meaning of a liberal arts education, and as a result they graduate students who are trained but not educated. And how many people are going to wade through a four hundred page book to discover basic principles about the mindset of the Founding Fathers' generation?

I envisioned this short work as a simple primer on the subject, and as such it was written for a general audience. For some people it will be nothing more than a reminder of what they already know, but for others I hope this essay will shed light on the uniqueness of the Founders' vision and the magnitude of our responsibility in maintaining the freedom that they bequeathed to us.

I wrote this with my sons Garrett, Griffin, and Graham in mind, because it is their generation, and those that follow, that will suffer the consequences if we forget. As usual, my wife, Jayne, has provided unflinching support and sage advice during my work on this project. Retired political science professor Connie Mauney volunteered her time and more importantly her keen eye to give this essay a thorough critique. I also acknowledge and thank Clay Young of Vision Creative & Marketing for his insights and crucial guidance in making this publication a reality. Finally, I wish to thank Lipscomb University, a place where academic freedom still flourishes and where students are developed in both mind and heart.

"Concentrated power has always been the enemy of liberty."

★ ★

- RONALD REAGAN

PART

1

THE PROBLEM

★ ★ ★ ★ ★ ★ ★ ★ ★ ★

★ BRITISH HERITAGE ★

Throughout the centuries a common theme in the development of civilizations is the concentration of power. Much of human history involves this familiar and recurring story, an effort to centralize power in the hands of a few governing elites or more often into the hands of one person. Call the supreme ruler what you wish–pharaoh, king, dictator, czar–it is accomplished through centralized authority and the ability to exert control over individuals and groups. When such political structures exist, power emanates from government, and personal liberty is restricted to that which the government is willing to grant. That is to say, liberty is limited, and subjects do as they are told while expressing gratitude for whatever favors, freedoms, rights, and benefits their ruler allows. This is the formula for tyranny.

By the eighteenth century the British Empire was different. Much of its political power was still vested in the hands of a monarch, but England's monarchical system had been transformed during the course of the seventeenth century. The primary agents of transformation were the English people who were notoriously unsubmissive and quick to challenge authority. As one historian put it, they "made poor subjects for monarchy, and they were proud of it." Indeed the English were an independent people who historically cherished their liberty. The events that significantly changed England's monarchical system were the English Civil War and the Glorious Revolution. In both cases, the British got rid of a king who had attempted to exercise too much power.[1]

The English Civil War was a series of armed clashes between supporters of Parliament and supporters of King Charles I. The king sought to concentrate power by binding Anglicanism on all of his Protestant subjects. In addition, he married a Catholic, which had religious implications for future monarchs. Believing in "divine right rule" (chosen by God and thus infallible) and unable to govern with Parliament's cooperation, Charles I simply tried to rule without it. For over a decade he refused to call Parliament into session. Without Parliament to appropriate money, Charles had to seek funds through unscrupulous methods, a stunning illustration of unprincipled cunning that heads of government will use to further their quest for power. Two examples will suffice. Unable legally to introduce new taxes, he simply expanded the ship tax to the entire population, even though it had been intended to apply only to coastal residents. Through another method he acquired money by having people arrested just so they would have to pay fines to get out of jail. During his reign tens of thousands of immigrants migrated to North America to escape his oppressive rule. After years of conflict, the king's efforts to usurp power resulted in his trial for treason followed by his execution in 1649, thus providing a lesson for future monarchs who tried to exert absolute rule.

When James II ascended to the throne four decades later, friction again arose between king and Parliament over religion and military policy. James's determination to rule without Parliament gives credence to the admonition of a German philosopher named Hegel: "We learn from history that we never learn anything from history." What followed was the Glorious Revolution in 1688, resulting in James's abdication and exile in France and Parliament's subsequent invitation to William and Mary to assume the throne of England. These events elevated the status of Parliament to the extent that it marked the beginning of a parliamentary democracy. Parliament's assertion of the power of the purse and the passage of a Bill of Rights limited future monarchs by requiring that they obtain Parliamentary approval in the exercise of certain powers. Absolute rule in England ended in favor of constitutional limits on the monarchy through law.

Thus, during the course of the seventeenth century, Englishmen had repeatedly confronted a monarch's effort to practice arbitrary rule without regard for the people's representatives, and in so doing they had succeeded in checking the power of the monarchy. Limited or constitutional monarchy allowed Englishmen to obtain a level of freedom uncommon in Europe. It also reinforced the notion that power ultimately resides with the people not the king, giving real meaning to the concept of English liberty.

The colonists living in North America were first and foremost Englishmen. They read the same kinds of material and they shared the same history with their counterparts across the ocean. They also shared the common trait or tendency toward independent thought and resistance to political authority. Whether in England or North America, Englishmen took pride in their independence. However, unlike tenant farming which prevailed in England, most colonists owned their own land, making their independence more deeply felt. It is important when tracing events that led to the American Revolution to remember that George Washington, Benjamin Franklin, John Adams, Thomas Jefferson and all of the other colonists of the Revolutionary War generation were Englishmen. They loved their country, knew its history, and championed its constitutional foundation. Knowing British history emboldened them in the 1760s and 1770s to confront unwelcome attempts to concentrate power with as much determination as had their countrymen a century earlier.

★ COLONIAL THOUGHT ★

Four decades after Lexington and Concord, John Adams wrote to Thomas Jefferson reflecting on those heady days when they both were young men caught up in the swirl of revolution. "What do we mean by the Revolution?" Adams asked. Then he went on to express an understanding of those transforming events that unfortunately is lost today. The Revolution was not the war with England that started when 700 British regulars opened fire on 77 Massachusetts militiamen at Lexington Green on April 19, 1775. Far from it–the revolution had already occurred before the guns and powder and blood. "The Revolution was in the minds of the people," Adams continued, "and this was affected, from 1760 to 1775, in the course of fifteen years before a drop of blood was shed at Lexington." The fighting was merely a "consequence" of the revolution. The revolution was not in the way the colonists viewed the role of government. They had a firm grasp of government's responsibility from their reading of Enlightenment writers and from a knowledge of their own history. Rather, the revolution was in their allegiance to their government.

Judging from what they read, it is obvious that the colonists drank deeply from the outpouring of Enlightenment thought that had flowed from the pens of political philosophers during the previous century. Harvard historian Bernard Bailyn painstakingly researched these political writings and their affect on the colonists and wrote a Pulitzer Prize winning book entitled, *The Ideological Origins of the American Revolution.* His book demonstrates that what influenced the Revolutionary War generation most were not concerns about class or wealth, rather it was about limiting the ever encroaching powers of government. It was that familiar story from history about government's concentration of power which, if unchecked, ultimately erodes liberty. Among the most influential of the many writers with whom the colonists were familiar were Thomas Hobbes, John Milton, John Locke, Algernon Sidney, John Trenchard and Thomas Gordon–all Englishmen except the Scotsman Gordon.[2]

Two important thoughts emerged from these Enlightenment political philosophers that played a significant role in the American Revolution: the Social Contract and Natural Rights. Succinctly stated, the Social Contract theory holds that government, to fulfill its function, must possess a degree of power. So, people entrust their government with sufficient power to maintain order, but with the understanding that government will not abuse the powers granted to it. In return, the people willingly submit themselves to government's authority, understanding that ultimately government is submissive to their will.[3] If, however, government attempts an unwanted or illegal expansion of its powers, it has broken the Social Contract, giving the people the right to do away with it and replace it with something different. In 1689 Locke explained why King James II had been removed from power in favor of William and Mary. He had broken the Social Contract. The same monarchical violation had also occurred with Charles I, who was beheaded for the offense.

The colonists were also intimately familiar with Natural Rights philosophy which resonated from many of the Enlightenment writers. To trace its origin we need to go back to the Scientific Revolution of the sixteenth and seventeenth centuries when men like Galileo, Copernicus, and Newton discovered the laws that govern planetary motion, the law of gravity, etc. Out of the Scientific Revolution came the idea that there are natural laws, put in place by God, that govern the universe. Those laws are permanent, fixed, and unchangeable. A century later it was easy for the political philosophers of the Enlightenment to go one step further in arguing that if there are natural laws that govern the universe, surely there must also be natural rights that are universal, granted by God, and undeniable by man. Locke asserted that among these God-given rights were life, liberty, and property. The Social Contract and Natural Rights were deeply embedded in English history, and they became central ideas in the Declaration of Independence.

The two writers who had perhaps the greatest influence on the mid-eighteenth century colonists were John Trenchard and Thomas Gordon who together wrote a series of essays called *Cato's Letters*. The pseudonym Cato was from the first century defender of republicanism and the adversary of Julius Caesar. Trenchard and Gordon wrote and published their essays in the 1720s, in the aftermath of the South Sea Bubble, a financial scandal involving the dishonest dealings of politicians along with the national bank in a private business. The colonists were eminently familiar with *Cato's Letters*, and at the heart of the essays were constant reminders of the corrupting nature of government power.

The lessons Cato taught are applicable in all ages for they speak to the very nature of government, which, regardless of its form, is conducted by humans. Thus Cato warned, "The world is governed by men, and men by their passions; which, being boundless and insatiable, are always terrible when they are not controuled." In another essay Cato advised that "Considering what sort of a creature man is, it is scarce possible to put him under too many restraints, when he is possessed of great power." Cato reminded them (and us) that governments by their nature tend toward aggressive, oppressive expansion of power. Conversely, "Liberty," Cato asserted, "chastises and shortens power, therefore power would extinguish liberty." In other words, individual liberty is the enemy of government power; thus uncontrolled government will seek to destroy liberty. A brief sampling of quotes from Cato's writings will suffice to give the flavor of the lessons taught.

- "Power, without control, appertains to God alone; and no man ought to be trusted with what no man is equal to. . . . The only security which we can have that men will be honest, is to make it their interest to be honest; and the best defence which we can have against their being knaves, [dishonest or unscrupulous] is to make it terrible to them to be knaves."

- "There is no evil under the sun but what is to be dreaded from men, who may do what they please with impunity: they seldom or never stop at certain degrees of mischief when they have power to go further."

- "Men that are above all fear, soon grow above all shame."

- "The people, when they are in the wrong, are generally in the wrong through mistake; and when they come to know it, are apt frankly to correct their own faults. . . . But it is not so with great men, and the leaders of parties; who are, for the most part, in the wrong through ambition, and continue in the wrong through malice. Their intention is wicked, and their end criminal."

- "The people, rightly managed, are the best friends to princes; and, when injured and oppressed, the most formidable enemies."

- "Power is like fire; it warms, scorches, or destroys, according as it is watched, provoked, or increased."

- "Unjust and unfrugal ways of throwing away money, make wicked and violent means necessary to get money; and rapine [taking property by force] naturally follows prodigality. They that waste publick money, seldom stop there, but go a wicked step farther; and having first drained the people, at last oppress them."

- "If therefore we would look for virtue in a nation, we must look for it in the nature of government."[4]

By the middle of the eighteenth century the colonists had a clear understanding of the exercise of power which can be summed up as follows. The concentration of power is a common theme in all ages of history. Men, once they have a degree of power, seek more, and by the concentration of power they then put themselves above the law. Governmental power and individual liberty cannot coexist--they operate in different spheres. Knowing these things, therefore, government's power must be well defined, and carefully confined, because governments by nature tend to expand their power. "Power is naturally active, vigilant, and distrustful," said Cato. Liberty, on the other hand, is passive and delicate and must be guarded lest it be gobbled up by government's insatiable appetite for control.

★ RESISTING TYRANNY ★

What the colonists learned from their reading was that government's exercise of power can easily become excessive. What they learned from their own experiences after 1763 was that it could actually happen to them. In that watershed year, they began to see evidence of unrestrained government aimed at their freedom and liberty. The French and Indian War, fought mostly in North America, had come to an end. Although England had won the war, the nation was deeply in debt, and it sought to remedy its financial woes.[5] King George III issued a proclamation restricting the colonists' westward movement, thereby limiting expenditures for frontier defense. The Mother Country also took steps to enforce long ignored trade laws. In 1764, Parliament passed the Sugar Act designed to first reduce and then strictly enforce the tax on molasses as well as bring greater regulation to colonial trade. Some of the money generated from the new law was to help pay the financial burden of permanently maintaining troops in the colonies. The presence of British Redcoats served as a symbol of the king's power and was an ominous sign of his intentions.

The Sugar Act sounded the alarm, but Parliament was not finished. That legislation was quickly followed by the Stamp Act (1765), which sought to raise revenue by taxing newspapers, licenses, legal documents, playing cards, and other types of paper products. It marked the first time that Parliament attempted to levy a direct tax on the colonies, and the act produced a firestorm of opposition. The colonists were accustomed to paying taxes levied by their colonial governments, but not those levied by Parliament. That it represented "taxation without representation" was a major but only secondary concern.

The real threat was an encroaching government that sought to exert its powers in unprecedented ways. The colonists had enjoyed increasing levels of independence over the years. Some of it admittedly came as a result of their own enterprising ways of avoiding tariffs and trade regulations, but much of it resulted from latitude and leniency intentionally granted through "salutary neglect." But the king now sought to reassert monarchical control to rein in his wayward colonies and to circumvent limits placed on the monarchy eighty years earlier by the Bill of Rights. The colonists held allegiance to their local assemblies and colonial governments and paid taxes to support colonial administration, but they sensed that the Mother Country was now attempting to make them vassals. This was a familiar theme down through history–a government of men (king and Parliament) attempting to usurp its authority over the people. The colonists would have none of it.

Their liberties as Englishmen rested on the firmly held principles of representation and consent. The actions of king and Parliament lent credence to the warnings that Cato and others had issued about the "clinching fist" of government power that, if unchecked, would crush liberty in its tyrannical grasp. As John Adams once put it, "British liberties are not the grants of princes and parliaments." Bernard Bailyn aptly summed up the situation: The colonists "saw about them, with increasing clarity, . . . evidence of nothing less than a deliberate assault launched surreptitiously by plotters against liberty." From history and from Enlightenment writers, colonists had learned that "what lay behind every political scene, the ultimate explanation of every political controversy, was the disposition of power."[6] Taxation was only a byproduct of the real problem, or, to put it differently, taxation was but a symptom of the disease of power.

Resistance took various forms, and one was an outpouring of opposition publications. Writers like James Otis sprang to action. In *The Rights of the British Colonies Asserted and Proved* (1764), Otis effectively argued that rights come from God and are not bestowed by government, and also that representation was a natural (God given) right. These were consistent themes echoed by Thomas Jefferson a decade later when he affirmed that the rights of a free people are "derived from the laws of nature, and not as the gift of their chief magistrate." Otis also asserted that "all laws and all taxations which bind the whole must be made by the whole." Thus came the argument "no taxation without representation."

As the protest grew, nine of the thirteen colonies passed resolutions that declared Parliament's attempts to tax them as violations of both the English constitution and their rights. In the Virginia House of Burgesses Patrick Henry, speaking against the Stamp Act, referred to his "Countrys Dying liberty." In August 1765, an angry crowd of Bostonians burned in effigy the local stamp distributor, Andrew Oliver, ransacked his house, and forced him to resign. Two weeks later rowdy protesters pillaged and damaged the home of Massachusetts' Lieutenant Governor Thomas Hutchinson for his determination to enforce the Stamp Act. By year's end the newly formed Sons of Liberty intensified their demonstrations and intimidations. In 1766 in Norfolk, Virginia, a man accused of being an informant for customs officials was tarred and feathered before being thrown into the ocean. A Stamp Act Congress declared that Parliament did not have the authority to levy a direct, or internal, tax on the colonies. These examples constitute but a sampling.

The widespread resistance created the Stamp Act Crisis. The riots, the intimidation of stamp collectors, the avalanche of printed proclamations in newspapers, resolutions, handbills, etc. in opposition to the measure took British officials by surprise. Tax agents were never able to effectively collect the Stamp Act revenues and within a year Parliament repealed the legislation. Augustus Henry FitzRoy, the duke of Grafton, and member of the House of Lords thought he knew why the Stamp Act had failed. There are a lot of ways to tax America, he counseled, just "don't tax them universally. By that means you join them when you should keep them asunder."[7] In other words, tax only certain segments or classes but not everyone. That way those not taxed will not protest, and those taxed will not be numerous enough to force change. And the most beneficial aspect of the duke's suggestion was that taxing only portions of society will effectively divide people.

Despite the firestorm, England forged ahead without heeding the warnings. Many of the British elites regarded the protesters as rabble and wayward children who did not know their place. (Whether one regarded opponents of these new government measures as "the people" or "a mob" depended entirely upon perspective, and advocates of government power must of necessity portray resisters in a negative light.) Parliament dismissed the constitutional argument that the colonists made about lack of representation by declaring that Parliament exercised "virtual" representation over the entire empire. Despite protests, England not only disregarded the colonists but persisted with different types of taxes and regulations. In turn colonial resistance intensified, bringing to mind another of Cato's warnings: "The first principles of power are in the people, . . . and whoever will pretend to govern them without regarding them, will soon repent it."

The colonists felt perfectly justified in resisting the Mother Country's attempts to expand its power. It was well-known that one of the warning signs that a potential tyrant was attempting to consolidate power was by trying to "levy taxes without popular consent." Furthermore, John Locke had warned that if an innocent man is forced to give that which belongs to him to someone who demands it in order to keep the peace, then "Robbers and Oppressors will be the only ones who will benefit." In addition, Algernon Sidney said regarding government excesses, it is "better that the . . . excesses of a prince should be restrained or suppressed, than that whole nations should perish by them." The colonists also understood, instinctively, that potential oppressors who are not resisted the first time they reach for power will attempt further oppressions later. They knew that the degree to which government's encroaching power could be restrained depended on the amount of energy the people could exert to keep it in check. So demonstrations continued, and those who stood ready to defend liberty were frequently accused of "advocating disorder."[8]

Boston was a whirlwind of discontent, and two clashes in 1770 led to bloodshed. In February Ebenezer Richardson, an unpopular customs official and secret informant for the lieutenant governor, confronted an angry crowd of boys and young men who had gathered near his home. He cut down an effigy that had been strung up and while attempting to take down a liberty pole, they attacked him. He fired into the crowd wounding one and killing Christopher Snider, a twelve-year-old boy. Richardson would be tried and convicted of murder, but later pardoned by the king. Watching Snider's funeral procession, John Adams concluded that "the Ardor of the People is not to be quelled by the Slaughter of one Child and the Wounding of another."[9]

The following month the famous Boston Massacre occurred when British soldiers fired into a crowd of demonstrators and killed five of them. Although the protesters were mostly white, one of the dead was a black man named Crispus Attucks. When the soldiers went on trial, John Adams suffered the wrath of his compatriots by offering to serve as their defense attorney. He did so because he wanted to demonstrate to observers in London that British officials could receive a fair trial in America and that the colonists were, in fact, the true protectors of law and constitutionalism.

Several points should be noted in regard to the defiance that emerged in America during the 1760s. First, the primary objective of the colonial leaders was not separation and independence, and those terms should not be confused with pleas for liberty. When they complained about the loss of liberty or when Patrick Henry cried "give me liberty or give me death," they were talking about their rights as Englishmen. As they saw it, the overriding problem was that their government in London did not regard the constitution as a limit to its power, and the colonists' objective was the restoration of constitutional law. Thus, rights, not independence, was the goal in the early going.

Second, despite well-publicized instances to the contrary, the resistance movement was predominately nonviolent. As the distinguished MIT historian Pauline Maier demonstrated in *From Resistance to Revolution*, to the extent that community leaders attained some degree of local organization, it was "in part to contain disorder." The so-called radicals were greatly concerned with law and order (thus Adams' willingness to provide legal counsel for the British soldiers after the Boston Massacre). Boston rioters would not even turn out to protest on Saturdays and Sundays because those were religious days.

Third, the various protests were spontaneous and therefore had no

organizational hierarchy. They occurred only in proportion to their disillusion-
ment with the Mother Country's policies. Actually, the uprisings were not all
that radical but were consistent with British history and with established colonial
traditions. Beginning with Bacon's Rebellion in 1676, by the mid-1700s significant popular uprisings had occurred in Connecticut, Massachusetts, New Jersey,
North Carolina, South Carolina, Pennsylvania, and Virginia.[10] So protesting
government action was not really new.

★ FROM RESISTANCE ★ TO INDEPENDENCE

By the 1770s, however, the ongoing conflict with England began to produce
a change of sentiments as thoughts began to shift from liberty to separation.
Parliament unwittingly set in motion a famous and serious chain of events when
it passed the Tea Act in May 1773. Believing that the huge but struggling East
India Company was too big to fail, the legislation was essentially a government
bailout. The company had fallen on hard financial times and had been unable to
obtain loans from the Bank of London. So it agreed to a reorganization that gave
government officials administrative oversight, and in return Parliament gave the
company a monopoly on the sale of tea in the colonies. The net result of the financial jockeying actually reduced the price of tea for colonists, but the Tea Act
also reiterated Parliament's assertion that it had the authority to levy taxes on
them. Parliament had provided a splendid example of the old adage that oppression is based on fear and favor–in other words, intimidation for those who resist
power and privilege for those whose patronage is needed to prop up power.

Events began to move swiftly now. When the first shipment of tea arrived in
Boston harbor in November 1773, angry Bostonians, intent on defending liberty,
staged an open act of defiance. Dubbed the Boston Tea Party, they boarded
the British ships on December 16, smashed several hundred crates of tea, and
dumped it into the harbor. It was an electrifying event. John Hancock later said,

"No one circumstance could possibly have taken place more effectively to unite the Colonies than this manouvre of the Tea."[11] The showdown had commenced and the ultimate outcome would determine who was actually in charge: the people or the government.

Shocked by the colonists' brazen actions, Parliament quickly responded by passing the Coercive Acts, which were designed to do exactly what the name suggests. These punitive measures did several things including closing the port of Boston, changing the colonial charter of Massachusetts, and regulating the way colonial officials were tried. In 1774 colonial resistance intensified up and down the continent, including nonimportation and nonconsumption of British goods. By fall, twelve colonies had sent fifty-six delegates to meet in Philadelphia in what became known as the First Continental Congress. Creating the Continental Congress resulted from two imperatives. One was the need to organize this massive resistance, and the other was to ensure that radicals bent on violence did not take control of the movement. This provides an American example of a common pattern in history. Resistance rises spontaneously, but at some point it has must organized to be effective.

Soon the Continental Congress passed unanimously the Suffolk Resolves, a set of defiant resolutions, which, in addition to effectively nullifying portions of the Coercive Acts, resolved to withhold taxes, and begin military preparations. The Suffolk Resolves acknowledged George III as the "rightful sovereign" of the colonies, but also asserted that such laws which violate colonial rights will not be obeyed. Note the change that had taken place in colonial thinking. When the turmoil first began in the mid-1760s, colonists professed loyalty to both the crown and to Parliament.

Now only a decade later, but after a long train of abuses and usurpations, the colonists were no longer willing to acknowledge Parliament's authority over them. Their only connection to the empire was through the king, the very embodiment of their government, in whom they depended for a redress of their grievances. The king, however, decided on a military solution to a political problem. He declared that the colonists were in a state of rebellion, and in April 1775, when British troops marched out of Boston to seize military supplies the colonists had gathered in Concord, they exchanged fire with local militia in Lexington. The opening shots of the Revolution had been fired.

Still many colonists as well as members of the Continental Congress remained committed to working out a solution with the king, insisting that they were both the loyal subjects of George III and at the same time the true defenders of British rights. They were willing to fight for liberty but not yet willing to define liberty in terms of independence. Meanwhile, most colonists held out hope that their differences with England might yet be resolved through negotiations. And those who, by this time, dared to talk about separation and independence did so in a whisper, for such ideas remained radical even as late as 1774 and 1775.

Then along came Thomas Paine and his little book *Common Sense*. In it Paine argued that there were two tyrannies in England: monarchy and aristocracy. He went on to champion equality by arguing that the distinction between a monarch and his subjects is a false one, and he explained how monarchs had caused more problems than they had solved. England and America did not have common interests, and it simply did not make sense for an island to rule a continent, Paine argued. He advocated independence in an effective and straightforward manner, and his argument spread like wildfire. *Common Sense* was published in January 1776 and it sold 120,000 copies in three months; half a million within a year–and at a time when the total population in the thirteen colonies was only 2.5 million. It was the most important publication of the period in convincing Americans that separation from England was simply a matter of common sense.

In spring 1776, building momentum for independence forced a discussion of the topic in the Continental Congress. What had been a radical notion just a few months earlier was championed throughout the colonies. In June Congress debated a resolution submitted by Virginia delegate Richard Henry Lee: "That these United Colonies are, and of right ought to be, free and independent States, that they are absolved from all allegiance to the British Crown, and that all political connection between them and the State of Great Britain is, and ought to be, totally dissolved." Congress voted for independence on July 2 and two days later, after making revisions, voted to adopt as their official statement Thomas Jefferson's famous document.

The Declaration of Independence was the colonists' justification for the unusual step they were taking. It was their explanation to the world, and it included their list of grievances. The document was clearly the result of Enlightenment influences, particularly that of John Locke. When Jefferson mentioned "unalienable rights" it was a reference to natural rights that everyone understood to be God-given or "sacred and immutable" as Jefferson wrote in the original draft. Or as Jefferson had put it two years earlier, "The God Who gave us life gave us liberty at the same time." Thus, the Declaration states, "We hold these truths to be self-evident, that all men are created equal, that they are endowed by their Creator with certain unalienable rights, that among these are life, liberty and the pursuit of happiness." Locke had talked of "life, liberty and property," but one might surmise that Jefferson equated property rights with the pursuit of happiness.

In that one sentence Jefferson provided the essence of what America has been about for more than two centuries: liberty and equality. Liberty meant the right to live one's life without government interference and equality was a reference to opportunity. (It is absurd to contend that Jefferson was referring to equality of outcome.) These two principles are at the heart of our nationhood. The country has not always lived up to those principles but they have been a part of our national fabric from the beginning, pushing the country forward. They were borrowed by Abraham Lincoln in 1863 when he spoke in dedication of the Union soldiers who died at Gettysburg. "Four score and seven years ago," he said, "our fathers brought forth on this continent a new nation, conceived in liberty and dedicated to the proposition that all men are created equal." Then Lincoln eloquently went on to profess that the Civil War was a test to see if a nation founded on such principles could endure. Yes, those principles articulated by Jefferson in 1776 goaded the nation until it abolished slavery.

Next, Jefferson explained the remedy that had been clearly established by Enlightenment writers in England during the previous century. "That to secure these rights, governments are instituted among men, deriving their just powers from the consent of the governed. That whenever any form of government becomes destructive to these ends, it is the right of the people to alter or to abolish it, and to institute new government, laying its foundation on such principles and organizing it powers in such form, as to them shall seem most likely to effect their safety and happiness." There, in a nutshell, was the social contract. Because the Mother Country had been usurping its authority and governing in a way that was destructive to American liberty and happiness, it had broken its covenant with the people. Now, just as England had done twice in the seventeenth century, the colonists were determined to create for themselves a new and better government.

One final point about the Declaration: it was addressed to the king. After the introductory paragraphs, the document contains a long list of grievances that all begin with the pronoun "He." Having already rejected Parliament's authority over them, all that remained was a justification for breaking with the king. The king was the last thread that held the colonies in the empire. In declaring their independence, the colonists had to show just cause for invoking the social contract and breaking that last thread. The complaints spanned a broad gamut, but a few examples will suffice.

-For placing conditions on the passage of laws Jefferson charged: "He has refused to pass other laws for the accommodation of large districts of people, unless suspended in their operation till his assent should be obtained."

-For interfering with the judicial process Jefferson charged: "He has made judges dependent on his will alone, for the tenure of their offices, and the amount and payment of their salaries."

-For enlarging the government bureaucracy Jefferson charged: "He has erected a multitude of new offices, and sent hither swarms of officers to harass our people, and eat out their substance."

-For violating the British constitution Jefferson charged: "He has combined with others to subject us to a jurisdiction foreign to our constitution, and unacknowledged by our laws; giving his assent to their acts of pretended legislation."

-And not until well down the list does the reader come to: "For imposing taxes on us without our consent."

Jefferson concluded the Declaration by "appealing to the Supreme Judge of the world" to determine "the rectitude of our intentions." He then restated the resolution that Congress had adopted on July 2 by announcing the colonies' break from England and declaring them to be "free and independent states." Then he invoked a "firm reliance on the protection of Divine Providence," and bound all those who signed to "mutually pledge to each other our lives, our fortunes and our sacred honor."

The people had met the problem head on and they had adopted a dangerous course. Declaring independence would surely bring more bloodshed as the Americans (no longer colonists) started down an uncertain road that would lead to no one knew where. But as Thomas Gordon argued in the early 1700s, popular uprisings may lead to anarchy, but anarchy was preferable to government tyranny. Anarchy, he said, would "do less harm" and would "end sooner" than the oppression that is brought about by tyranny. "Tyranny may last for ages, and go on destroying, till at last it has nothing to destroy."[12] To borrow a line from Abraham Lincoln's second inaugural address, "and the war came."

NOTES

1. Gordon Wood, *The Radicalism of the American Revolution* (New York: Alfred A. Knopf, 1992), pp. 12-16, quote on 13.

2. Bernard Bailyn, *The Ideological Origins of the American Revolution* (Cambridge: Harvard University Press, 1967, paperback ed., 1980), chapter 2, especially pp. 35-36.

3. Some people believe that the Social Contract theory actually originated during the Protestant Reformation in the sixteenth century. It is the idea that the Protestant notion of a covenant relationship wherein God and Christians have mutual obligations were applied to government and the governed.

4. John Trenchard and Thomas Gordon, *Cato's Letters: or Essays on Liberty, Civil and Religious, and Other Important Subjects*, edited by Ronald Hamowy, (Indianapolis: Liberty Fund, 1995), vol. 1 pp. 156, 175, 176, 179, 186, 189, 198, 222, 234, 237, 238, 239, 240.

5. England's national debt in 1763 stood at □122,603,336 and growing. Robert Middlekauff, *The Glorious Cause: The American Revolution, 1763-1789* (New York: Oxford University Press, 1982), p. 57.

6. Bailyn, *The Ideological Origins of the American Revolution*, pp. 55, 96.

7. Harry M. Ward, *The American Revolution: Nationhood Achieved, 1763-1788* (New York: St. Martin's Press, Inc., 1995), pp. 33-37, quotes on p. 35.

8. Pauline Maier, *From Resistance to Revolution: Colonial Radicals and the Developemnt of American Opposition to Britain, 1765-1776* (New York: Random House, 1972, Vintage paperback ed., 1972), pp. 31-46.

9. Ward, *The American Revolution*, pp. 41-42.

10. Maier, *From Resistance to Revolution*, pp. xi-xii, xv, 12-13, 25. Maier's book, especially chapters one and two, contributed significantly to this study's assertions regarding resistance.

11. Ward, *The American Revolution*, pp. 44-46.

12. Maier, *From Resistance to Revolution*, p. 42.

PART
2

THE SOLUTION

★ ★ ★ ★ ★ ★ ★ ★ ★ ★

★ GEORGE WASHINGTON ★ AND POWER

If the problem is encroaching government power, the solution is devising a system that effectively restrains government. After declaring their independence, Americans experienced a "trial and error" process before arriving at a workable arrangement. Before moving on to the events that led to our Constitution, one topic from the Revolutionary War years wants notice. It does not recount battles and campaigns, but it does bear on the issue at hand.

George Washington's conduct as commander-in-chief of the Continental Army offers valuable insights into the proper use of power and the attainment of greatness. How is it that a general who lost most of the battles ended up winning the war? And how is it that such a general, having come close to being ousted from power in the second year of the war because of his failures, could emerge at war's end as the most admired, respected, and revered man on the continent? Indeed, Americans call him the Father of the Country. These questions are answered by a brief look at how Washington used the power entrusted to him.

George Washington was not a military genius; however, he possessed an astute mind when it came to observation, judgment, and adaptability. He learned valuable lessons from the disappointing loss of New York City to the British in 1776. Losing one of the most important American cities only two months after declaring their independence was a disaster that seemed to signal the failure of the Revolution. But Washington learned, changed his strategy, and never again fought the British on their terms. He persevered, traded space for time, kept his army in the field, and eventually turned a rag-tag collection of poorly trained militia into a respectable army that, with the help of the French, succeeded in handing the British one of its greatest embarrassments of the war at Yorktown in 1781. It was the last battle of the war and Washington's first major victory. He demonstrated what North Vietnamese General Vo Nguyen Giap confirmed two centuries later: you can lose the battles but win the war.

Among the many obstacles that challenged General Washington was the Continental Congress which never adequately fed, clothed, or equipped the army. Members of Congress argued and debated to the extent that they often rendered the body feeble and inept. By the end of the war, the legislative body had almost lost all credibility at home and abroad. Washington had volunteered to serve the army and the country without a salary, and by the time the war ended eight years later he had lost half of his net worth. In contrast, some members of Congress had become rich from the conflict. Despite his constant frustrations with the bickering and often incompetent politicians and despite the fact that while they debated, his soldiers went without pay, food, and shoes, the general never tried to thwart civilian control and authority over the military.

Washington's leadership abilities and judicious use of power are nowhere more evident than in the closing months of the war while the army was encamped at Newburgh, New York awaiting the completion of the peace treaty. Disgruntled officers, angry at Congress's inability to pay them, began to talk of "throwing the bums out" and perhaps replacing Congress with a military government headed by their much respected commander, General Washington. The true intention of the plotters has never been definitively determined, but it was clear that this so-called Newburgh Conspiracy involved something extra-legal and perhaps even sinister. This type of thing has happened often in history and has always constituted one of the great threats to a free people. A victorious general emerges as a strong man, and in uncertain times succeeds in using the devotion of the people to take over the reins of government.

How would Washington respond to such a test? When he learned what was afoot, he acted immediately to put an end to their "disorderly proceedings." Walking in unexpectedly at an officers' meeting, Washington read a prepared statement. He told them not to take a course of action that, when "viewed in the calm light of reason, will lessen the dignity and sully the glory you have hitherto maintained." He pleaded with them to have "confidence in the purity of the intentions of Congress." Again he referred to "the dignity of your conduct" and the "glorious example" they had previously set, and he cautioned them to bear in mind the image they would leave to posterity. The officers sat in silence for five minutes as the general softly but firmly rebuked their actions. The plot was quashed.[1]

Take advantage of a crisis to achieve unprecedented power? Perhaps become a military dictator? George Washington refused, and in so doing he demonstrated that he knew the difference between power honorably wielded and power derived from lust and opportunity. When the war officially ended in fall 1783, Washington demonstrated once again an ability to walk away from power. With the signing of the Treaty of Paris, the British army that occupied New York City boarded their ships and sailed away in November. It had been seven years since the Continental Army's embarrassing and near disastrous abandonment of the city. Now Washington marched back in as a triumphant general. He had persevered and now was alone the most respected man in the country. He was universally popular–not in the wild, frenzied sense that is often observed in modern times with popular actors, musicians, and the like, but a dignified popularity for one who had truly accomplished something meaningful.

At the peak of his popularity and power he said goodbye to his army and within two weeks was in Annapolis, Maryland, the temporary seat of government. Unknown to members of Congress, Washington at the pinnacle of success had come to resign his commission as commanding general. His intention was to do what few expected and still fewer would have the will to do–refuse power. He went to see Thomas Mifflin, the president of Congress, and asked to speak before that legislative body. Ironically, Mifflin had been on Washington's staff early in the war but became disenchanted with slow promotion and critical of Washington's leadership. Subsequently, he participated in the Conway Cabal, a scheme in 1777-1778 to oust Washington as commander of the army. Washington knew of Mifflin's role in the plot and their meeting was icy–cordial but formal.

Nonetheless, Mifflin granted Washington's request, and three days later the general stood before a hushed assemblage and read a prepared statement. Understanding the historic weight of what he was doing, the paper shook in his hand as he read. He thanked Congress for its support during the war. Then he said that in achieving the new nation's objectives he had relied on "the patronage of Heaven" and he expressed his "gratitude for the interposition of Providence." He read on: "I consider it as indispensable duty to close this last solemn act of my official life by commending the Interests of our dearest Country to the protection of Almighty God." Here, according to one observer, his voice broke. "Having now finished the work assigned me, I retire from the great theater of action . . . I here offer my Commission, and take my leave of all the employments of public life." With that, Washington took a paper from his coat pocket. Firmly holding the commission that Congress had given him in 1775 that appointed him commander-in-chief of the Continental Army, he walked over and handed it to Mifflin.[2]

For a second time in 1783 George Washington walked away from power, and in doing so cemented his place in history. When King George asked an American in London what Washington would do after the war, the man answered that he would probably go back home to his Virginia farm. "If he does that," said the astonished king, "he will be the greatest man in the world." Americans agreed. Thomas Jefferson described Washington thus: "He was, in every sense of the words, a wise, good, and great man" and "never did nature and fortune combine more perfectly to make a man great." Four decades after Washington's death, Daniel Webster said, "America has furnished to the world the character of Washington. And if our American institutions had done nothing else, that alone would have entitled them to the respect of mankind." Abraham Lincoln described him this way: "Washington is the mightiest name on earth." "To add brightness to the sun, or glory to the name of Washington, is alike impossible."

George Washington understood what few leaders in history have grasped: the willingness to give up power is a true sign of greatness. To grasp for power, as the colonists saw it, was to side with tyranny and oppression, but to walk away from it was a mark of virtue and character. It was Montesquieu, a French political philosopher during the Enlightenment, who said, "To become truly great, one has to stand with people, not above them." Finally, it was perhaps while reflecting on Washington that Jefferson later said, "Power is not alluring to pure minds."

★ A First Draft: The Articles ★ of Confederation

Americans revolted against the old world of monarchy. They turned their backs on a system where men governed arbitrarily in favor of a system that allowed them to live free. They would rule themselves rather than be ruled. As Alexander Hamilton from New York wrote, "The only distinction between freedom and slavery consists in this: In a state of freedom, a man is governed by the laws to which he has given his consent, either in person, or by his representative. In a state of slavery, he is governed by the will of another." As preeminent Constitutional historian Forrest McDonald put it, our Founding Fathers understood that "the essence of tyranny was the unrestrained expression of the will of the sovereign–that is, whoever it was that had the power to make and enforce the law."[3] Monarchy and aristocracy, power and privilege would not hold sway in the new world that the Founders were building. Fear and favor would not define superior/subordinate relationships, nor would birth, inheritance, and favoritism. They intended to establish a meritocracy where merit, talent, and preparation determine one's fate and hard work determines success. They knew that luck rarely shines on the indolent, but is most often found where preparation and hard work meet.

Winning their independence allowed Americans an opportunity to put to use what they learned from history and Enlightenment writings. Their effort to reshape government was in essence a marriage between literature and politics. By the time the Revolutionary War ended, Congress already had a framework of government in place which had been ratified by the thirteen states. The Articles of Confederation was a first draft attempt at a solution to the problem of government. It lasted scarcely more than a decade. Much of the framework made sense if one takes into account the fears and experiences of the preceding two decades, but like all first drafts, it needed improvements.

In keeping with its name, confederation, meaning a group of independent entities that combine to form a loose union, the new government maintained at its core the sovereignty of the thirteen states. Article II: "Each state retains its sovereignty, freedom and independence, and every Power, Jurisdiction and right, which is not by this confederation expressly delegated to the United States, in Congress assembled." Article III referred to the new nation as "a firm league of friendship" by which the various states agreed to act in concert in matters of defense, securing of liberties, and resisting attacks on religion, sovereignty and trade. The main purpose for this decentralized, states rights structure was to prevent unwanted concentrations of power at the national level. It guaranteed that the nexus of political power would be at the state level, which would insure that the most important political decisions would be decided more or less locally. It also reflected the common belief that representative governments work best in a small geographic area.

So great was their fear of government's inevitable concentration of power that they intentionally created a blueprint for weak national government. Thomas Jefferson echoed what many of his generation believed: "Most bad government has grown out of too much government." The confederation government had but one branch–legislative–and it was unicameral. Regardless of the number of representatives a state sent to Congress, it had only one vote. With no judicial branch the highest courts in the land resided at the state level, and no executive branch meant no chief executive officer. Having just gone through a series of conflicts with the king, Americans were disinclined to create a system that placed too much power in the hands one individual. The potential for abuse was too great.

Given recent experience, the Founding Fathers refused to grant to the new national government the power to tax. It could only request annual contributions from the states, but without any coercive power, it could not force the states to comply. The framers were willing to entrust such a potentially destructive power only to the states, which were more susceptible to local control. The state governments liked the arrangement, but it is hardly the stuff of which solvent governments are made. In this case it was a fatal weakness considering the staggering debt that the new nation had accumulated by war's end. The amount, about $54 million, seems but a drop in the bucket by today's standards, but two centuries ago it was sufficiently enormous to threaten to overwhelm the young government.

Other weaknesses, both structural and procedural, bore witness to the Founding Father's hyper concern for limited government. For example, the Confederation government had no regulatory powers over commerce, and the articles could not be amended except by unanimous consent. With all of the safeguards and limits that defined the new government, Americans could be confident that governmental excesses and despotism would not arise from the ashes of the old British colonies (at least at the national level). But would this new framework suffice to provide order and security? In their zeal to ensure that their new government would be limited, Americans were overzealous.

Several difficulties beset the Confederation government, but the issue that nearly sank the ship of state was the debt. Attempts to gain approval for import duties to raise revenue failed as did efforts to reorganize the debt. In summer 1786, Rufus King, a member of the Massachusetts congressional delegation, wrote, "the Treasury now is literally without a penny." Three months later, a tax revolt known as Shays' Rebellion erupted in Massachusetts in opposition to, among other things, the state government's level of taxing and spending. In fact, during the confederation years numerous states had begun to oppress its citizens through taxation and regulation, a development of which Shays' Rebellion was but an example. Ominous signs abounded that the country was sinking into anarchy, which in turn produced urgent calls for a convention to determine how to bring order out of the chaos that seemed to be overwhelming the nation.

★ A NEW FRAMEWORK ★ FOR GOVERNMENT

When fifty-five delegates met in Philadelphia in 1787, their paramount concern was how to strengthen the national government while keeping it limited. Their objective was to grant the authority necessary to ensure its permanence and solvency while ensuring that it lacked the power to become despotic? Establishing a stable, effective government that will not over reach for power and control was, for the Framers, the great dilemma. What they came up with was a masterpiece.

It is generally assumed that the Constitutional Convention was an exercise in increasing governmental power. It was not. It was an exercise in reorganizing government to bring order, consistency, and permanent limits to its power. The Framers did not seek nor did they create new forms of governmental power that did not previously exist. Rather they shuffled powers that already existed at the national and state levels, taking some functions that only states had been allowed to exercise (like the power to tax) and sharing it with the new government. In other words, without creating any new powers they simply reordered those which already existed. Or as James Madison (the Father of the Constitution) explained in Federalist 45, the new Constitution had less to do in adding new power "than in the invigoration of its original powers." The net result was a new and more centralized government, stronger than the confederation government and with sufficient power to guarantee nationhood–but with strict limits.

In creating this governmental system, the Framers were always cognizant of how they might bind the new government so as to keep it under control. They intended to keep it limited by forcing it into the confines of the law–that law being the Constitution itself. A few years later Thomas Jefferson emphatically put it like this, with only slight exaggeration, "The two enemies of the people are criminals and government, so let us tie the second down with the chains of the Constitution so the second will not become the legalized version of the first." One must remember that the Constitution was written to govern government not people. It is the chain that holds government down, the high wall if you will, that keeps it in check. It is the safeguard that keeps government in its proper sphere so that individual liberty will not be threatened. In other words, the Constitution was actually written to defend people from government. That is why so much of the Constitution was written in the negative, telling government what it may not do. Thus, approximately twenty percent of the document's text stipulates what is not permissible for the government to do while only eleven percent of the text makes specific grants of power.[4]

The central features of the new governmental framework were federalism (the distribution of power between the central government and the states) and separation of powers (three branches within the federal government). Dividing power into so many parts was an important ingredient in keeping government limited. Montesquieu was the primary advocate for separation of powers, and Madison was greatly influenced by his writing. With three co-equal branches, each with its own unique responsibilities, coupled with an intricate set of checks and balances, no single branch would be able to exert excessive power. The potential for congressional abuse is kept in check by the threat of a presidential veto as well as the judicial review prerogative of the judiciary. Federal judges sit on the bench only by presidential appointment which in turn must win Senate approval. The president cannot make laws, nor can the judiciary. That power resides solely with the legislative branch. Federal officeholders are subject to impeachment. On and on go the checks that the various branches have on each other, guaranteeing Constitutional limits on power. The only way to circumvent effectively its legal limits would be if all three branches were in league to do so.

One of the most significant debates at the convention had to do with the creation of an executive branch, and this brings us back to George Washington. There was disagreement over an executive office for the same reason that no such office existed under the Articles of Confederation. Too few people were willing to entrust that much power to one person, which would be reminiscent of monarchy. However, the deciding factor was Washington's presence in Philadelphia. After considerable coaxing he had reluctantly agreed to leave Mount Vernon and attend the convention where the delegates selected him as the presiding officer. Washington rarely participated in the debates, but while others went back and forth negotiating various points, he sat there overseeing the discussions and elevating the prestige of the occasion by his mere presence.

When it came to debating the creation of an executive branch and the office of the presidency, the doubters needed only to look to the presiding official at the head of the room and recall his careful stewardship of power a few years earlier. For everyone present knew that if they created a presidency, George Washington would be the first to hold the office. Would he violate the people's trust? Would he seek greater authority than had been conferred upon him? Would he attempt to concentrate power under his control? No! They all knew that power (and liberty) was safe in his hands. Thus, the expression: "It was not what Washington did that made him great but who he was."

The Constitution was the result of four months of discussion, debate, and compromise by fifty-five men who, while disagreeing on many of the particulars, in the end accomplished their objective. They had engineered a new government framework capable of providing stability but with enough tethers to keep the new creation in check. Each branch would be answerable to the others and the whole answerable to the people. Even the legislative branch would be restrained by the rule of law. The Founders made lawmaking a slow, involved, and sometimes complicated process: slow so that laws could not be passed in the dark of night without the people's knowledge and complicated so that there would be ample opportunities for a bill to be killed in the process. The Constitution helps safeguard the people by making it difficult to pass laws. As the Founders envisioned, laws should be not only carefully scrutinized, but they should be few in number and simple in design. As Montesquieu expressed it, "Useless laws weaken the necessary laws." In their wisdom, the Founders created gridlock to save the people from excessive governing.

Two major concerns posed hurdles to the Constitution's ratification. One was the fear that the states would be subordinated and subjugated by an unnecessarily powerful federal government. Madison wrote Federalist 45 to allay those fears. In it he reminded readers that under the Constitution the powers of the federal government are "few and defined. . . . [and] will be exercised principally on external objects, as war, peace, negotiation, and foreign commerce." In fact, Madison contended, it will only be during such times of national peril as war that there will be a temporary "ascendancy" of the federal government over the states. While federal powers are limited, those "reserved to the several States will extend to all objects which, in the ordinary course of affairs, concern lives, liberties, and properties of the people, and the internal order, improvement, and prosperity of the State."

The other hurdle was in a desire for a Bill of Rights to guarantee certain cherished liberties like freedom of speech, the press, and religion. In fact, some people made their support of ratification conditional on the promise of a Bill of

Rights, and so proponents of ratification committed to provide such protections as soon as the new government was in place. And indeed a Bill of Rights, in the form of ten amendments, was added straightway to the Constitution. However, this addition worried some people, and their concern should be a warning to us. Skeptics believed that since the Constitution afforded no powers to the new federal government except those expressly granted, no partial listing of rights was necessary, and that to do so would actually weaken rather than strengthen personal liberty. Alexander Hamilton, a New York delegate to the convention, warned in Federalist 84 that listing in a bill of rights "various powers not granted . . . would afford a . . . pretext to claim more than were granted." Pennsylvanian James Wilson likewise asserted that it would be folly to start listing the rights that Americans enjoy because it would be impossible to list them all, and in time people would assume that anything not on the list was not a right. Regarding freedom of the press Charles Cotesworth Pinckney of South Carolina, in wondering about the necessity of the First Amendment said that since the federal "government has no powers but what are expressly granted to it; it therefore has no power to take away the liberty of the press."[5]

Unfortunately, it seems that Hamilton, Wilson, and Pinckney were correct. Some people now believe that American rights consist only of those listed in the Bill of Rights. It is generally forgotten today that the federal government is authorized to exercise only the powers expressly granted in the Constitution, and that the Bill of Rights is not an exhaustive list of the liberties that Americans possess. It is also today a too common misconception that the government is the dispenser of rights. This fundamental misunderstanding can be found in government officials as well as a misinformed citizenry, and it lends itself to the unhealthy conclusion that the people are subservient to government rather than the other way around. This sad fact brings to mind the assertion that the nineteenth century Frenchman Alexis de Tocqueville made in *Democracy in America* that government's ability to consolidate power and subjugate its people is in direct proportion to that people's level of ignorance.

There is one more point to make regarding amendments. After the convention George Washington admitted that the Constitution was not a perfect document. It was, however, the best they could create and, no doubt, far superior to anything that subsequent generations could have come up with. The Framers of the Constitution were enlightened but not Divinely inspired. They knew that changes and additions would be needed over time to reflect a changing society. So, they provided a mechanism for it–the amendment process. The Constitution should not be viewed as a "living document" that can be changed at the whim of a judge under the influence of public pressure. Subjecting the meaning of the document to such arbitrary opinions infuses the process with that which the Framers tried to keep out of it–politics. If the Constitution needs to be changed and a large percentage of the population agrees that it should, the document's creators provided the means.

★ SLAVERY IN THE CONSTITUTION ★

In its finished form, the Constitution did not encompass all that the various delegates hoped for. It was too liberal for some and too conservative for others, but at the end of the process, it was an ingenious product designed to be broad enough to be acceptable to South Carolinians and Virginians as well as Pennsylvanians and New Yorkers. The one major accommodation that northern delegates grudgingly made to southerners had to do with slavery. It was the price of union.

Specifically, there were two items that dealt with the slave issue, although the topic was not mentioned by name in the document. One dealt with the importation of slaves from Africa and is found in Article I, Section 9: "The Migration or Importation of such Persons as any of the States now existing shall think proper to admit, shall not be prohibited by the Congress prior to the year one thousand eight hundred and eight. . . ." The underlying intention of this section has been inaccurately portrayed by critics as a desire on the part of the Founders to safeguard the international slave trade for at least the next twenty years following the convention. That they wanted to protect the slave trade surely must be a sign of their hypocrisy. Actually, it was a compromise that put southerners on notice that the heinous practice of importing slaves would not be guaranteed forever. To ensure that some of the southern delegates did not bolt the convention, they were thus given this temporary reprieve to continue the importation of slaves, but with the implication that after twenty years, there would be no such guarantee. Indeed, the slave trade was outlawed in 1808 as northern delegates hoped and intended.

The other item, which has been more universally abused, deals with how slaves were to be counted in apportioning seats in the House of Representatives, and is found in Article I, Section 2: Representatives will be apportioned among the states "according to their respective Numbers, which shall be determined by adding to the whole Number of free Persons, including those bound to Service for a Term of Years, and excluding Indians not taxed, three fifths of all other Persons." It is the famous Three-fifths Compromise. Critics contend that the compromise demonstrates that the Founders did not consider slaves to be fully human because each slave could be counted as only three-fifths of a person. This falsehood is widely disseminated in our schools and elsewhere. The provision allowed for three-fifths (60%) of the total number of slaves in a state to be counted toward that state's population total–a big difference. It has nothing to do with degrees of humanity.

It was simply another compromise that northern delegates made as an undesirable cost associated with keeping the thirteen states together. Delegates from the northern free states who opposed slavery did not want to count the slaves at all. Counting slaves would give the less populated slave states an unfair boost in Congressional representation, and northern delegates thought it preposterous to count people who were not citizens and could not vote. On the other hand, southern delegates saw including slaves as a way to gain an artificial increase in representation, thereby helping to offset their population disparity with the North. They wanted all of their slaves counted. (The compromise increased the percentage of House seats held by the slave states from 41% to 46%.) Consider this. If the critics' version is correct, and the Three-fifths Compromise actually reflects the Founders' beliefs about a slave's level of humanity, think about who the heroes and villains would be. The heroes would be the southern slaveholders who wanted to count all slaves, and the villains would be the anti-slavery northerners who wanted them to count as zero.

Slavery was the grand contradiction of the age. It was the great injustice that ran counter to the principles of the Revolutionary War–liberty and equality. Many of the Founders deplored the institution of slavery. John Adams said, "Every measure of prudence, therefore, ought to be assumed for the eventual total extirpation of slavery from the United States. . . . I have, through my whole life, held the practice of slavery in . . . abhorrence." Benjamin Franklin clearly stated that "Slavery is . . . an atrocious debasement of human nature." Even some southern slaveowners came to acknowledge the wickedness of the institution. Patrick Henry admitted that even though "I deplore slavery, I see that prudence forbids its abolition." Jefferson was as conflicted as any slaveholder over what to do: "We have the wolf by the ears, and can neither hold him, nor safely let him go. Justice is in one scale, and self-preservation in the other." Washington said, "There is not a man living who wishes more sincerely than I do, to see a plan adopted for the abolition of [slavery]." And he ultimately took his own words to heart, freeing his slaves at his death and providing them with financial assistance from his estate.

The new republic did succeed in putting slavery on the road to extinction. When the Framers met in Philadelphia, it had been eleven years since Jefferson wrote the Declaration of Independence, and already six states had provided for the abolition of slavery and others would soon follow. When the first census was taken in 1790 (three years after the Constitutional Convention), there were 27,000 free blacks in the North and 32,000 in the South. Twenty years later there were 78,000 in the North and 108,000 in the South. The trend was due largely to a burgeoning abolition and manumission movement in the southern slave states.[6] But alas, the ultimate extermination of slavery would take much longer and come at a greater cost than any of the Founders could have imagine.

★ THE INDISPENSABLE INGREDIENT ★

As already noted the Constitution did not create new government power; rather it succeeded in reordering the power that already existed. The new federal government was strengthened and stabilized but within an apparatus that would keep it under control. At Philadelphia the Founders succeeded in limiting government by dividing it, checking it, balancing it, and effectively confining it within defined boundaries of law. It was, as one historian put it, "a limited government under law." It was intended to be so limited that Gouverneur Morris, a Pennsylvania delegate, wondered if the new government would have enough business to conduct to warrant meeting every year. By intentionally keeping government limited they sought to leave the people the widest possible range of liberty. Indeed, in the system they created the people are sovereign.

However, and this, reader, is the crucial factor, the degree to which limited government can work depends upon the degree to which people can govern themselves. Therefore, self-government depends upon what Forrest McDonald called the "life-giving principle of republics," which is virtue, the essential element upon which rests the viability of representative government. As Richard Brookhiser put it, "the first form of self-government is governing ourselves."[7] That is why one cannot peruse the writings of the Founders without constantly stumbling across references to virtue. Not long after the Constitutional Convention adjourned James Madison shared a common belief when he wrote, "To suppose that any form of government will secure liberty or happiness without any virtue in the people is a chimerical [delusional] idea." Note that when they used the term they were not just referring to moral behavior and Christian values, though that was part of it. Rather, they more often meant "public virtue" which carries the meaning of corporate responsibility or civic duty.

Often thought of as civic virtue, those who exhibit such traits willingly subjugate personal desires to the good of the whole, not because it is the law but because it is the responsible and wholesome thing to do. Liberty is perpetuated only through virtuous living and virtuous living is the result of lifestyle habits. Civic virtue is defined by the following characteristics: self-discipline, independence, self-sufficiency, hard-work, and frugality. A society that exhibits these characteristics needs and wants little government. However, the society that is ruled by passions, impulse, avarice, greed, covetousness, materialism, and prodigality and where a sizeable percentage of the population games the system and goes on the public dole, that society needs and, sad to say, wants much government.

The adage "with freedom comes responsibility" has been so often repeated that it seems like merely a cliché, but its simple truth is vital. At the time of the founding, American society and culture generally expected its citizens to be self-sufficient and hard working not just because it was good for the individual but because to do otherwise would be a burden to the community. When Alexis de Tocqueville traveled through the United States in the early nineteenth century, he clearly observed this interplay between individual liberty and societal responsibility. "No one in the United States has pretended that, in a free country, a man has the right to do everything; on the contrary, more varied social obligations have been imposed on him than elsewhere; no one thought to attack the very basis of social power or contest its rights." Later Tocqueville explained that even though "the law allows the American people to do everything, there are things which religion prevents them from imagining and forbids them to dare." Limited government provides liberty not license.

Understanding the role of virtue in a free society forces an acknowledgment of the role of religion in the ideological world of the Revolutionary War generation, admittedly an unpopular topic today. The notion that religious beliefs played a part in the founding of the country has been demonized for decades. However, the argument that religious convictions did not play a role is a historical fallacy. To be sure, the Founders did not want nor did they create a theocracy, but they clearly understood that religion is the wellspring of morality and virtue, or as Richard Henry Lee put it, "Religion is the guardian of morals." The following quote from Tocqueville describes his observations about religion that is not mandated by law but is nevertheless a powerful force in society: "Religion, which never intervenes directly in the government of American society, should therefore be considered as the first of their political institutions, for although it did not give them the taste for liberty, it singularly facilitates their use thereof."[8]

Knowing these precepts about virtue in a limited government gives clear meaning to the following quotes. John Adams wrote, "We have no government armed with power capable of contending with human passions unbridled by morality and religion. Our Constitution was made only for a moral and religious people. It is wholly inadequate to the government of any other." James Madison echoed the same theme: "We have staked the whole future of American civilization, not upon the power of government, far from it. We have staked the future of all of our political institutions upon the capacity of mankind for self-government; upon the capacity of each and all of us to govern ourselves, to control ourselves, to sustain ourselves according to the Ten Commandments of God."

Finally, no greater advice can be offered in the twenty-first century than that which was left to posterity by the Father of the Country in his farewell address. It is unfortunate that modern-day students are so rarely exposed to this important document, and more unfortunate that so few secondary school history teachers seem to know of its existence. In his last official communication to his fellow countrymen, Washington gave perceptive advice that is even more needed today than it was two centuries ago. He warned that the manipulation of political parties "serves always to distract the public councils and enfeeble the public administration. It agitates the community with illfounded jealousies and false alarms; kindles the animosity of one part against another. . . ." Regarding a national debt he cautioned that public credit should be used sparingly, "avoiding likewise the accumulation of debt . . . not ungenerously throwing upon posterity the burden which we ourselves ought to bear." And concerning the conduct of individuals in a free society, he imparted this wisdom: "Of all the dispositions and habits which lead to political prosperity, religion and morality are indispensable supports. In vain would that man claim the tribute of patriotism who would labor to subvert these great pillars of human happiness. . . . Reason and experience both forbid us to expect that national morality can prevail in exclusion of religious principle. . . . virtue and morality is a necessary spring of popular government."

We conclude the narrative where we began. A consistent theme through the ages is the tendency of governments to concentrate power. It has happened many times in history, and it always comes at the expense of personal liberty. Too often power succeeds by filling the void left when virtue disappears. Thomas Jefferson's words still ring true: "The issue today is the same as it has been throughout all history, whether man shall be allowed to govern himself or be ruled by a small elite." At the conclusion of the Constitutional Convention, a woman is said to have approached Benjamin Franklin and asked, "What have you given us?" to which he responded, "A republic, if you can keep it."

NOTES

1. Washington's Newburgh speech is quoted in Willard Sterne Randall, *George Washington: A Life* (New York: Henry Holt and Company, Inc., 1997), p. 396. For portions of Washington's resignation that follows, see pp. 400-09.

2. The full text of Washington's resignation speech to Congress is on the Maryland State Archives: www.msa.md.gov.

3. Forrest McDonald and Ellen Shapiro McDonald, *Requiem: Variations on Eighteenth-Century Themes* (Lawrence: The University Press of Kansas, 1988), pp. 25, 35. Forrest McDonald began his career in the 1950s by debunking Charles Beard's economic interpretation of the Constitution, and remains one of the foremost constitutional historians of the last half century.

4. Ibid., pp. 19-20. The McDonalds disagree with some of my views but their work is fascinating and brilliant. Various sections of this essay draw especially from chapters one and two.

5. Forrest McDonald, *States' Rights and the Union: Imperium in Imperio, 1776-1876* (Lawrence: The University Press of Kansas, 2000), p. 23.

6. Interested readers should consult Thomas G. West's important book *Vindicating the Founders: Race, Sex, Class, and Justice in the Origins of America* (New York: Rowman & Littlefield Publishers, Inc. 1997), pp. 5-11. This study draws from other parts of chapter one as well.

7. McDonald and McDonald, *Requiem*, p. 17. The quote beginning "the first form" is from Richard Brookhiser, *Founding Father: Rediscovering George Washington* (New York: Free Press, 1996), p. 193.

8. Alexis de Tocqueville, *Democracy in America*, trans. George Lawrence (New York: Harper & Row, 1988), vol. I, p. 292.

APPENDIX

The
Declaration
of Independence

★ ★ ★ ★ ★ ★ ★ ★ ★ ★ ★ ★ ★

The
United States
Constitution

Declaration of Independence

When, in the course of human events, it becomes necessary for one people to dissolve the political bands which have connected them with another, and to assume among the powers of the earth, the separate and equal station to which the laws of nature and of nature's God entitle them, a decent respect to the opinions of mankind requires that they should declare the causes which impel them to the separation.

We hold these truths to be self-evident, that all men are created equal, that they are endowed by their Creator with certain unalienable rights, that among these are life, liberty and the pursuit of happiness. That to secure these rights, governments are instituted among men, deriving their just powers from the consent of the governed. That whenever any form of government becomes destructive to these ends, it is the right of the people to alter or to abolish it, and to institute new government, laying its foundation on such principles and organizing its powers in such form, as to them shall seem most likely to effect their safety and happiness. Prudence, indeed, will dictate that governments long established should not be changed for light and transient causes; and accordingly all experience hath shown that mankind are more disposed to suffer, while evils are sufferable, than to right themselves by abolishing the forms to which they are accustomed. But when a long train of abuses and usurpations, pursuing invariably the same object evinces a design to reduce them under absolute despotism, it is their right, it is their duty, to throw off such government, and to provide new guards for their future security. --Such has been the patient sufferance of these colonies; and such is now the necessity which constrains them to alter their former systems of government. The history of the present King of Great Britain is a history of repeated injuries and usurpations, all having in direct object the establishment of an absolute tyranny over these states. To prove this, let facts be submitted to a candid world.

He has refused his assent to laws, the most wholesome and necessary for the public good.

He has forbidden his governors to pass laws of immediate and pressing importance, unless suspended in their operation till his assent should be obtained; and when so suspended, he has utterly neglected to attend to them.

He has refused to pass other laws for the accommodation of large districts of people, unless those people would relinquish the right of representation in the legislature, a right inestimable to them and formidable to tyrants only.

He has called together legislative bodies at places unusual, uncomfortable, and distant from the depository of their public records, for the sole purpose of fatiguing them into compliance with his measures.

He has dissolved representative houses repeatedly, for opposing with manly firmness his invasions on the rights of the people.

He has refused for a long time, after such dissolutions, to cause others to be elected; whereby the legislative powers, incapable of annihilation, have returned to the people at large for their exercise; the state remaining in the meantime exposed to all the dangers of invasion from without, and convulsions within.

He has endeavored to prevent the population of these states; for that purpose obstructing the laws for naturalization of foreigners; refusing to pass others to encourage their migration hither, and raising the conditions of new appropriations of lands.

He has obstructed the administration of justice, by refusing his assent to laws for establishing judiciary powers.

He has made judges dependent on his will alone, for the tenure of their offices, and the amount and payment of their salaries.

He has erected a multitude of new offices, and sent hither swarms of officers to harass our people, and eat out their substance.

He has kept among us, in times of peace, standing armies without the consent of our legislature.

He has affected to render the military independent of and superior to civil power.

He has combined with others to subject us to a jurisdiction foreign to our constitution, and unacknowledged by our laws; giving his assent to their acts of pretended legislation.

For quartering large bodies of armed troops among us.

For protecting them, by mock trial, from punishment for any murders which they should commit on the inhabitants of these states.

For cutting off our trade with all parts of the world.

For imposing taxes on us without our consent.

For depriving us in many cases, of the benefits of trial by jury.

For transporting us beyond seas to be tried for pretended offenses.

For abolishing the free system of English laws in a neighboring province, establishing therein an arbitrary government, and enlarging its boundaries so as to render it at once an example and fit instrument for introducing the same absolute rule in these colonies.

For taking away our charters, abolishing our most valuable laws, and altering fundamentally the forms of our governments.

For suspending our own legislatures, and declaring themselves invested with power to legislate for us in all cases whatsoever.

He has abdicated government here, by declaring us out of his protection and waging war against us.

He has plundered our seas, ravaged our coasts, burned our towns, and destroyed the lives of our people.

He is at this time transporting large armies of foreign mercenaries to complete the works of death, desolation and tyranny, already begun with circumstances of cruelty and perfidy scarcely paralleled in the most barbarous ages, and totally unworthy the head of a civilized nation.

He has constrained our fellow citizens taken captive on the high seas to bear arms against their country, to become the executioners of their friends and brethren, or to fall themselves by their hands.

He has excited domestic insurrections amongst us, and has endeavored to bring on the inhabitants of our frontiers, the merciless Indian savages, whose known rule of warfare, is undistinguished destruction of all ages, sexes and conditions.

In every stage of these oppressions we have petitioned for redress in the most humble terms: our repeated petitions have been answered only by repeated injury. A prince, whose character is thus marked by every act which may define a tyrant, is unfit to be the ruler of a free people.

Nor have we been wanting in attention to our British brethren. We have warned them from time to time of attempts by their legislature to extend an unwarrantable jurisdiction over us. We have reminded them of the circumstances of our emigration and settlement here. We have appealed to their native justice and magnanimity, and we have conjured them by the ties of our common kindred to disavow these usurpations, which, would inevitably interrupt our connections and correspondence. They too have been deaf to the voice of justice and of consanguinity. We must, therefore, acquiesce in the necessity, which denounces our separation, and hold them, as we hold the rest of mankind, enemies in war, in peace friends.

We, therefore, the representatives of the United States of America, in General Congress, assembled, appealing to the Supreme Judge of the world for the rectitude of our intentions, do, in the name, and by the authority of the good people of these colonies, solemnly publish and declare, that these united colonies are, and of right ought to be free and independent states; that they are absolved from all allegiance to the British Crown, and that all political connection between them and the state of Great Britain, is and ought to be totally dissolved; and that as free and independent states, they have full power to levy war, conclude peace, contract alliances, establish commerce, and to do all other acts and things which independent states may of right do. And for the support of this declaration, with a firm reliance on the protection of Divine Providence, we mutually pledge to each other our lives, our fortunes and our sacred honor.

NEW HAMPSHIRE:
JOSIAH BARTLETT, WILLIAM WHIPPLE, MATTHEW THORNTON

MASSACHUSETTS:
JOHN HANCOCK, SAMUEL ADAMS, JOHN ADAMS, ROBERT TREAT PAINE, ELBRIDGE GERRY

RHODE ISLAND:
STEPHEN HOPKINS, WILLIAM ELLERY

CONNECTICUT:
ROGER SHERMAN, SAMUEL HUNTINGTON, WILLIAM WILLIAMS, OLIVER WOLCOTT

NEW YORK:
WILLIAM FLOYD, PHILIP LIVINGSTON, FRANCIS LEWIS, LEWIS MORRIS

NEW JERSEY:
RICHARD STOCKTON, JOHN WITHERSPOON, FRANCIS HOPKINSON, JOHN HART, ABRAHAM CLARK

PENNSYLVANIA:
ROBERT MORRIS, BENJAMIN RUSH, BENJAMIN FRANKLIN, JOHN MORTON, GEORGE CLYMER, JAMES SMITH, GEORGE TAYLOR, JAMES WILSON, GEORGE ROSS

DELAWARE:
CAESAR RODNEY, GEORGE READ, THOMAS MCKEAN

MARYLAND:
SAMUEL CHASE, WILLIAM PACA, THOMAS STONE, CHARLES CARROLL OF CARROLLTON

VIRGINIA:
GEORGE WYTHE, RICHARD HENRY LEE, THOMAS JEFFERSON, BENJAMIN HARRISON, THOMAS NELSON, JR., FRANCIS LIGHTFOOT LEE, CARTER BRAXTON

NORTH CAROLINA:
WILLIAM HOOPER, JOSEPH HEWES, JOHN PENN

SOUTH CAROLINA:
EDWARD RUTLEDGE, THOMAS HEYWARD, JR., THOMAS LYNCH, JR., ARTHUR MIDDLETON

GEORGIA:
BUTTON GWINNETT, LYMAN HALL, GEORGE WALTON

The United States Constitution

We the People of the United States, in Order to form a more perfect Union, establish Justice, insure domestic Tranquility, provide for the common defense, promote the general Welfare, and secure the Blessings of Liberty to ourselves and our Posterity, do ordain and establish this Constitution for the United States of America.

ARTICLE I

Section 1. All legislative Powers herein granted shall be vested in a Congress of the United States, which shall consist of a Senate and House of Representatives.

Section 2. The House of Representatives shall be composed of Members chosen every second Year by the People of the several States, and the Electors in each State shall have the Qualifications requisite for Electors of the most numerous Branch of the State Legislature. No Person shall be a Representative who shall not have attained to the age of twenty five Years, and been seven Years a Citizen of the United States, and who shall not, when elected, be an Inhabitant of that State in which he shall be chosen.

Representatives and direct Taxes shall be apportioned among the several States which may be included within this Union, according to their respective Numbers, which shall be determined by adding to the whole Number of free Persons, including those bound to Service for a Term of Years, and excluding Indians not taxed, three fifths of all other Persons. The actual Enumeration shall be made within three Years after the first Meeting of the Congress of the United States, and within every subsequent Term of ten Years, in such Manner as they shall by Law direct. The Number of Representatives shall not exceed one for every thirty Thousand, but each State shall have at Least one Representative; and until such enumeration shall be made, the State of New Hampshire shall be entitled to choose three, Massachusetts eight, Rhode-Island and Providence Plantations one, Connecticut five, New-York six, New Jersey four, Pennsylvania eight, Delaware one, Maryland six, Virginia ten, North Carolina five, South Carolina five, and Georgia three.

When vacancies happen in the Representation from any State, the Executive Authority thereof shall issue Writs of Election to fill such Vacancies.

The House of Representatives shall choose their Speaker and other Officers; and shall have the sole Power of Impeachment.

Section 3. The Senate of the United States shall be composed of two Senators from each State, chosen by the Legislature thereof, for six Years; and each Senator shall have one Vote.

Immediately after they shall be assembled in Consequence of the first Election, they shall be divided as equally as may be into three Classes. The Seats of the Senators of the first Class shall be vacated at the Expiration of the second Year, of the second Class at the Expiration of the fourth Year, and the third Class at the Expiration of the sixth Year, so that one third may be chosen every second Year; and if Vacancies happen by Resignation, or otherwise, during the Recess of the Legislature of any State, the Executive thereof may make temporary Appointments until the next Meeting of the Legislature, which shall then fill such Vacancies.

No Person shall be a Senator who shall not have attained to the Age of thirty Years, and been nine Years a Citizen of the United States and who shall not, when elected, be an Inhabitant of that State for which he shall be chosen.

The Vice President of the United States shall be President of the Senate, but shall have no Vote, unless they be equally divided.

The Senate shall choose their other Officers, and also a President pro tempore, in the Absence of the Vice President, or when he shall exercise the Office of President of the United States.

The Senate shall have the sole Power to try all Impeachments. When sitting for that Purpose, they shall be on Oath or Affirmation. When the President of the United States is tried, the Chief Justice shall preside: And no Person shall be convicted without the Concurrence of two thirds of the Members present.

Judgment in Cases of Impeachment shall not extend further than to removal from Office, and disqualification to hold and enjoy any Office of Honor, Trust or Profit under the United States: but the Party convicted shall nevertheless be liable and subject to Indictment, Trial, Judgment and Punishment, according to Law.

Section 4. The Times, Places and Manner of holding Elections for Senators and Representatives, shall be prescribed in each State by the Legislature thereof; but the Congress may at any time by Law make or alter such Regulations, except as to the Places of choosing Senators.

The Congress shall assemble at least once in every Year, and such Meeting shall be on the first Monday in December, unless they shall by Law appoint a different Day.

Section 5. Each House shall be the Judge of the Elections, Returns and Qualifications of its own Members, and a Majority of each shall constitute a Quorum to do Business; but a smaller Number may adjourn from day to day, and may be authorized to compel the Attendance of absent Members, in such Manner, and under such Penalties as each House may provide.

Each House may determine the Rules of its Proceedings, punish its Members for disorderly Behavior, and, with the Concurrence of two thirds, expel a Member.

Each House shall keep a Journal of its Proceedings, and from time to time publish the same, excepting such Parts as may in their Judgment require Secrecy; and the Yeas and Nays of the Members of either House on any question shall, at the Desire of one fifth of those Present, be entered on the Journal.

Neither House, during the Session of Congress, shall, without the Consent of the other, adjourn for more than three days, nor to any other Place than that in which the two Houses shall be sitting.

Section 6. The Senators and Representatives shall receive a Compensation for their Services, to be ascertained by Law, and paid out of the Treasury of the United States. They shall in all Cases, except Treason, Felony and Breach of the Peace, be privileged from Arrest during their Attendance at the Session of their respective Houses, and in going to and returning from the same; and for any Speech or Debate in either House, they shall not be questioned in any other Place.

No Senator or Representative shall, during the Time for which he was elected, be appointed to any civil Office under the Authority of the United States, which shall have been created, or the Emoluments whereof shall have been increased during such time: and no Person holding any Office under the United States, shall be a Member of either House during his Continuance in Office.

Section 7. All Bills for raising Revenue shall originate in the House of Representatives; but the Senate may propose or concur with Amendments as on other Bills.

Every Bill which shall have passed the House of Representatives and the Senate, shall, before it become a Law, be presented to the

President of the United States; if he approve he shall sign it, but if not he shall return it, with his Objections to that House in which it shall have originated, who shall enter the Objections at large on their Journal, and proceed to reconsider it. If after such Reconsideration two thirds of that House shall agree to pass the Bill, it shall be sent, together with the Objections, to the other House, by which it shall likewise be reconsidered, and if approved by two thirds of that House, it shall become a Law. But in all such Cases the Votes of both Houses shall be determined by Yeas and Nays, and the Names of the Persons voting for and against the Bill shall be entered on the Journal of each House respectively. If any Bill shall not be returned by the President within ten Days (Sundays excepted) after it shall have been presented to him, the Same shall be a Law, in like Manner as if he had signed it, unless the Congress by their Adjournment prevent its Return, in which Case it shall not be a Law.

Every Order, Resolution, or Vote to which the Concurrence of the Senate and House of Representatives may be necessary (except on a question of Adjournment) shall be presented to the President of the United States; and before the Same shall take Effect, shall be approved by him, or being disapproved by him, shall be repassed by two thirds of the Senate and House of Representatives, according to the Rules and Limitations prescribed in the case of a bill.

Section 8. The Congress shall have Power To lay and collect Taxes, Duties, Imposts and Excises, to pay the Debts and provide for the common Defense and general Welfare of the United States; but all Duties, Imposts and Excises shall be uniform throughout the United States;

To borrow Money on the credit of the United States;

To regulate Commerce with foreign Nations, and among the several States, and with the Indian Tribes;

To establish an uniform Rule of Naturalization, and uniform Laws on the subject of Bankruptcies throughout the United States;

To coin Money, regulate the Value thereof, and of foreign Coin, and fix the Standard of Weights and Measures;

To provide for the Punishment of counterfeiting the Securities and current Coin of the United States;

To establish Post Offices and post Roads;

To promote the Progress of Science and useful Arts, by securing for limited Times to Authors and Inventors the exclusive Right to their respective Writings and Discoveries;

To constitute Tribunals inferior to the Supreme Court;

To define and punish Piracies and Felonies committed on the high Seas, and Offences against the Law of Nations;

To declare War, grant Letters of Marque and Reprisal, and make Rules concerning Captures on Land and Water;

To raise and support Armies, but no Appropriation of Money to that Use shall be for a longer Term than two Years;

To provide and maintain a Navy;

To make Rules for the Government and Regulation of the land and naval Forces;

To provide for calling forth the Militia to execute the Laws of the Union, suppress Insurrections and repel Invasions;

To provide for organizing, arming, and disciplining, the Militia, and for governing such Part of them as may be employed in the Service of the United States, reserving to the States respectively, the Appointment of the Officers, and the Authority of training the Militia according to the discipline prescribed by Congress;

To exercise exclusive Legislation in all Cases whatsoever, over such District (not exceeding ten Miles square) as may, by Cession of particular States, and the Acceptance of Congress, become the Seat of the Government of the United States, and to exercise like Authority over all Places purchased by the Consent of the Legislature of the State in which the Same shall be, for the Erection of Forts, Magazines, Arsenals, dock-Yards, and other needful Buildings;--And

To make all Laws which shall be necessary and proper for carrying into Execution the foregoing Powers, and all other Powers vested by this Constitution in the Government of the United States, or in any Department or Officer thereof.

Section 9. The Migration or Importation of such Persons as any of the States now existing shall think proper to admit, shall not be prohibited by the Congress prior to the Year one thousand eight hundred and eight, but a Tax or duty may be imposed on such Importation, not exceeding ten dollars for each Person.

The Privilege of the Writ of Habeas Corpus shall not be suspended, unless when in Cases of Rebellion or Invasion the public Safety may require it.

No Bill of Attainder or ex post facto Law shall be passed.

No Capitation, or other direct, Tax shall be laid, unless in Proportion to the Census or Enumeration herein before directed to be taken.

No Tax or Duty shall be laid on Articles exported from any State.

No Preference shall be given by any Regulation of Commerce or Revenue to the Ports of one State over those of another: nor shall Vessels bound to, or from, one State, be obliged to enter, clear or pay Duties in another.

No Money shall be drawn from the Treasury, but in Consequence of Appropriations made by Law; and a regular Statement and Account of Receipts and Expenditures of all public Money shall be published from time to time.

No Title of Nobility shall be granted by the United States: And no Person holding any Office of Profit or Trust under them, shall, without the Consent of the Congress, accept of any present, Emolument, Office, or Title, of any kind whatever, from any King, Prince, or foreign State.

Section 10. No State shall enter into any Treaty, Alliance, or Confederation; grant Letters of Marque and Reprisal; coin Money; emit Bills of Credit; make any Thing but gold and silver Coin a Tender in Payment of Debts; pass any Bill of Attainder, ex post facto Law, or Law impairing the Obligation of Contracts, or grant any Title of Nobility.

No State shall, without the Consent of the Congress, lay any Imposts or Duties on Imports or Exports, except what may be absolutely necessary for executing it's inspection Laws: and the net Produce of all Duties and Imposts, laid by any State on Imports or Exports, shall be for the Use of the Treasury of the United States; and all such Laws shall be subject to the Revision and Control of the Congress.

No State shall, without the Consent of Congress, lay any Duty of Tonnage, keep Troops, or Ships of War in time of Peace, enter into any Agreement or Compact with another State, or with a foreign Power, or engage in War, unless actually invaded, or in such imminent Danger as will not admit of delay.

ARTICLE II

Section 1. The executive Power shall be vested in a President of the United States of America. He shall hold his Office during the Term of four Years, and, together with the Vice President, chosen for the same Term, be elected, as follows:

Each State shall appoint, in such Manner as the Legislature thereof may direct, a Number of Electors, equal to the whole Number of Senators and Representatives to which the State may be entitled in the Congress: but no Senator or Representative, or Person holding an Office of Trust or Profit under the United States, shall be appointed an Elector.

The Electors shall meet in their respective States, and vote by Ballot for two Persons, of whom one at least shall not be an Inhabitant of the same State with themselves. And they shall make a List of all the Persons voted for, and of the Number of Votes for each; which List they shall sign and certify, and transmit sealed to the Seat of the Government of the United States, directed to the President of the Senate. The President of the Senate shall, in the Presence of the Senate and House of Representatives, open all the Certificates, and the Votes shall then be counted. The Person having the greatest Number of Votes shall be the President, if such Number be a Majority of the whole Number of Electors appointed; and if there be more than one who have such Majority, and have an equal Number of Votes, then the House of Representatives shall immediately choose by Ballot one of them for President; and if no Person have a Majority, then from the five highest on the List the said House shall in like Manner choose the President. But in choosing the President, the Votes shall be taken by States, the Representation from each State having one Vote; A quorum for this Purpose shall consist of a Member or Members from two thirds of the

States, and a Majority of all the States shall be necessary to a Choice. In every Case, after the Choice of the President, the Person having the greatest Number of Votes of the Electors shall be the Vice President. But if there should remain two or more who have equal Votes, the Senate shall choose from them by Ballot the Vice President.

The Congress may determine the Time of choosing the Electors, and the Day on which they shall give their Votes; which Day shall be the same throughout the United States.

No Person except a natural born Citizen, or a Citizen of the United States, at the time of the Adoption of this Constitution, shall be eligible to the Office of President; neither shall any Person be eligible to that Office who shall not have attained to the Age of thirty five Years, and been fourteen Years a Resident within the United States.

In Case of the Removal of the President from Office, or of his Death, Resignation, or Inability to discharge the Powers and Duties of the said Office, the Same shall devolve on the Vice President, and the Congress may by Law provide for the Case of Removal, Death, Resignation or Inability, both of the President and Vice President, declaring what Officer shall then act as President, and such Officer shall act accordingly, until the Disability be removed, or a President shall be elected.

The President shall, at stated Times, receive for his Services, a Compensation, which shall neither be increased nor diminished during the Period for which he shall have been elected, and he shall not receive within that Period any other Emolument from the United States, or any of them.

Before he enter on the Execution of his Office, he shall take the following Oath or Affirmation:--"I do solemnly swear (or affirm) that I will faithfully execute the Office of President of the United States, and will to the best of my Ability, preserve, protect and defend the Constitution of the United States."

Section 2. The President shall be Commander in Chief of the Army and Navy of the United States, and of the Militia of the several States, when called into the actual Service of the United States; he may require the Opinion, in writing, of the principal Officer in each of the executive Departments, upon any Subject relating to the Duties of their respective Offices, and he shall have Power to grant Reprieves and Pardons for Offences against the United States, except in Cases of Impeachment.

He shall have Power, by and with the Advice and Consent of the Senate, to make Treaties, provided two thirds of the Senators present concur; and he shall nominate, and by and with the Advice and Consent of the Senate, shall appoint Ambassadors, other public Ministers and Consuls, Judges of the supreme Court, and all other Officers of the United States, whose Appointments are not herein otherwise provided for, and which shall be established by Law: but the Congress may by Law vest the Appointment of such inferior Officers, as they think proper, in the President alone, in the Courts of Law, or in the Heads of Departments.

The President shall have Power to fill up all Vacancies that may happen during the Recess of the Senate, by granting Commissions which shall expire at the End of their next Session.

Section 3. He shall from time to time give to the Congress Information of the State of the Union, and recommend to their Consideration such Measures as he shall judge necessary and expedient; he may, on extraordinary Occasions, convene both Houses, or either of them, and in Case of Disagreement between them, with Respect to the Time of Adjournment, he may adjourn them to such Time as he shall think proper; he shall receive Ambassadors and other public Ministers; he shall take Care that the Laws be faithfully executed, and shall Commission all the Officers of the United States.

Section 4. The President, Vice President and all civil Officers of the United States, shall be removed from Office on Impeachment for, and Conviction of, Treason, Bribery, or other high Crimes and Misdemeanors.

ARTICLE III

Section 1. The judicial Power of the United States, shall be vested in one supreme Court, and in such inferior Courts as the Congress may from time to time ordain and establish. The Judges, both of the supreme and inferior Courts, shall hold their Offices during good Behavior, and shall, at stated Times, receive for their Services, a Compensation, which shall not be diminished during their Continuance in Office.

Section 2. The judicial Power shall extend to all Cases, in Law and Equity, arising under this Constitution, the Laws of the United States, and Treaties made, or which shall be made, under their Authority;--to all Cases affecting Ambassadors, other public Ministers and Consuls;--to all Cases of admiralty and maritime Jurisdiction;--to Controversies to which the United States shall be a Party;--to Controversies between two or more States;--between a State and Citizens of another State;--between Citizens of different States;--between Citizens of the same State claiming Lands under Grants of different States, and between a State, or the Citizens thereof, and foreign States, Citizens or Subjects.

In all Cases affecting Ambassadors, other public Ministers and Consuls, and those in which a State shall be Party, the Supreme Court shall have original Jurisdiction. In all the other Cases before mentioned, the Supreme Court shall have appellate Jurisdiction, both as to Law and Fact, with such Exceptions, and under such Regulations as the Congress shall make.

The Trial of all Crimes, except in Cases of Impeachment, shall be by Jury; and such Trial shall be held in the State where the said Crimes shall have been committed; but when not committed within any State, the Trial shall be at such Place or Places as the Congress may by Law have directed.

Section 3. Treason against the United States, shall consist only in levying War against them, or in adhering to their Enemies, giving them Aid and Comfort. No Person shall be convicted of Treason unless on the Testimony of two Witnesses to the same overt Act, or on Confession in open Court.

The Congress shall have Power to declare the Punishment of Treason, but no Attainder of Treason shall work Corruption of Blood, or Forfeiture except during the Life of the Person attainted.

ARTICLE IV

Section 1. Full Faith and Credit shall be given in each State to the public Acts, Records, and judicial Proceedings of every other State. And the Congress may by general Laws prescribe the Manner in which such Acts, Records, and Proceedings shall be proved, and the Effect thereof.

Section 2. The Citizens of each State shall be entitled to all Privileges and Immunities of Citizens in the several States.

A Person charged in any State with Treason, Felony, or other Crime, who shall flee from Justice, and be found in another State, shall on Demand of the executive Authority of the State from which he fled, be delivered up, to be removed to the State having Jurisdiction of the Crime.

No Person held to Service or Labor in one State, under the Laws thereof, escaping into another, shall, in Consequence of any Law or Regulation therein, be discharged from such Service or Labor, but shall be delivered up on Claim of the Party to whom such Service or Labor may be due.

Section 3. New States may be admitted by the Congress into this Union; but no new States shall be formed or erected within the Jurisdiction of any other State; nor any State be formed by the Junction of two or more States, or Parts of States, without the Consent of the Legislatures of the States concerned as well as of the Congress.

The Congress shall have Power to dispose of and make all needful Rules and Regulations respecting the Territory or other Property belonging to the United States; and nothing in this Constitution shall be so construed as to Prejudice any Claims of the United States, or of any particular State.

Section 4. The United States shall guarantee to every State in this Union a Republican Form of Government, and shall protect each of them against Invasion; and on Application of the Legislature, or of the Executive (when the Legislature cannot be convened) against domestic Violence.

ARTICLE V

The Congress, whenever two thirds of both Houses shall deem it necessary, shall propose Amendments to this Constitution, or, on the Application of the Legislatures of two thirds of the several States, shall call a Convention for proposing Amendments, which, in either Case, shall be valid to all Intents and Purposes, as Part of this Constitution, when ratified by the Legislatures of three fourths of the several States, or by Conventions in three fourths thereof, as the one or the other Mode of Ratification may be proposed by the Congress; Provided that no Amendment which may be made prior to the Year One thousand eight hundred and eight shall in any Manner affect the first and fourth Clauses in the Ninth Section of the first Article; and that no State, without its Consent, shall be deprived of its equal Suffrage in the Senate.

Article VI

All Debts contracted and Engagements entered into, before the Adoption of this Constitution, shall be as valid against the United States under this Constitution, as under the Confederation.

This Constitution, and the Laws of the United States which shall be made in Pursuance thereof; and all Treaties made, or which shall be made, under the Authority of the United States, shall be the supreme Law of the Land; and the Judges in every State shall be bound thereby, any Thing in the Constitution or Laws of any State to the Contrary notwithstanding.

The Senators and Representatives before mentioned, and the Members of the several State Legislatures, and all executive and judicial Officers, both of the United States and of the several States, shall be bound by Oath or Affirmation, to support this Constitution; but no religious Test shall ever be required as a Qualification to any Office or public Trust under the United States.

Article VII

The Ratification of the Conventions of nine States, shall be sufficient for the Establishment of this Constitution between the States so ratifying the Same.

Done in Convention by the Unanimous Consent of the States present the Seventeenth Day of September in the Year of our Lord one thousand seven hundred and Eighty seven and of the Independence of the United States of America the Twelfth

In witness whereof We have hereunto subscribed our Names,

GEORGE WASHINGTON
PRESIDENT AND DEPUTY FROM VIRGINIA

NEW HAMPSHIRE:
JOHN LANGDON, NICHOLAS GILMAN

MASSACHUSETTS:
NATHANIEL GORHAM, RUFUS KING

CONNECTICUT:
WILLIAM SAMUEL JOHNSON, ROGER SHERMAN

NEW YORK:
ALEXANDER HAMILTON

NEW JERSEY:
WILLIAM LIVINGSTON, DAVID BREARLY, WILLIAM PATERSON, JONATHAN DAYTON

PENNSYLVANIA:
BENJAMIN FRANKLIN, THOMAS MIFFLIN, ROBERT MORRIS, GEORGE CLYMER, THOMAS FITZSIMONS, JARED INGERSOLL, JAMES WILSON, GOUVERNEUR MORRIS

DELAWARE:
GEORGE READ, GUNNING BEDFORD, JR., JOHN DICKINSON, RICHARD BASSETT, JACOB BROOM

MARYLAND:
AMES MCHENRY, DANIEL OF SAINT THOMAS JENIFER,
DANIEL CARROLL

VIRGINIA:
JOHN BLAIR, JAMES MADISON, JR.

NORTH CAROLINA:
WILLIAM BLOUNT, RICHARD DOBBS SPAIGHT, HUGH WILLIAMSON

SOUTH CAROLINA:
JOHN RUTLEDGE, CHARLES COTESWORTH PINCKNEY,
CHARLES PINCKNEY, PIERCE BUTLER

GEORGIA:
WILLIAM FEW, ABRAHAM BALDWIN

"The contest for ages has been to rescue liberty from the grasp of executive power."

– DANIEL WEBSTER

★ ★ ★ ★ ★ ★ ★ ★ ★ ★ ★ ★ ★ ★ ★ ★ ★ ★ ★

"The people never give up their liberties but under some delusion."

– EDMUND BURKE

★ ★ ★ ★ ★ ★ ★ ★ ★ ★ ★ ★ ★ ★ ★ ★ ★ ★ ★

"History teaches us that grave threats to liberty often come in times of urgency, when constitutional rights seem too extravagant to endure."

– THURGOOD MARSHALL

★ ★ ★ ★ ★ ★ ★ ★ ★ ★ ★ ★ ★ ★ ★ ★ ★ ★ ★

"I believe there are more instances of the abridgment of the freedom of the people by gradual and silent encroachments of those in power than by violent and sudden usurpations."

– JAMES MADISON

★ ★ ★ ★ ★ ★ ★ ★ ★ ★ ★ ★ ★ ★ ★ ★ ★ ★ ★ ★

"Liberty has never come from the government. Liberty has always come from the subjects of it. The history of liberty is a history of resistance.

– WOODROW WILSON

★ ★ ★ ★ ★ ★ ★ ★ ★ ★ ★ ★ ★ ★ ★ ★ ★ ★ ★ ★

"There is danger from all men. The only maxim of a free government ought to be to trust no man living with power to endanger the public liberty."

– JOHN ADAMS

★ ★ ★ ★ ★ ★ ★ ★ ★ ★ ★ ★ ★ ★ ★ ★ ★ ★ ★ ★

*"Nations grown corrupt love bondage more than liberty;
bondage with ease rather than strenuous liberty."*

– JOHN MILTON

★ ★

*"Those who expect to reap the blessings of freedom,
must … undergo the fatigue of supporting it."*

– THOMAS PAINE

★ ★

*"Liberty means responsibility. That is why most
men dread it."*

– GEORGE BERNARD SHAW

★ ★

"The greatest dangers to liberty lurk in insidious encroachment by men of zeal, well-meaning but without understanding."

– LOUIS D. BRANDEIS

★ ★

Only vigilance and strength will deter tyranny.

– RONALD REAGAN

★ ★

"The natural progress of things is for liberty to yield and government to gain ground."

– THOMAS JEFFERSON

★ ★

"Liberty may be endangered by the abuse of liberty, but also by the abuse of power."

— JAMES MADISON

★ ★ ★ ★ ★ ★ ★ ★ ★ ★ ★ ★ ★ ★ ★ ★ ★ ★ ★

"The Founders knew that a democracy would lead to some kind of tyranny. The term democracy appears in none of our Founding documents. Their vision for us was a Republic and limited government."

— WALTER WILLIAMS

★ ★ ★ ★ ★ ★ ★ ★ ★ ★ ★ ★ ★ ★ ★ ★ ★ ★ ★

"Democracy is two wolves and a lamb voting on what to have for lunch. Liberty is a well-armed lamb contesting the vote."

— BENJAMIN FRANKLIN

★ ★ ★ ★ ★ ★ ★ ★ ★ ★ ★ ★ ★ ★ ★ ★ ★ ★ ★

NOTES